Pressed Flowers
in Miniature

NONA PETTERSEN

SEARCH PRESS

The Miniature View of the Urban Garden

All the flower arrangements in this book are based on a small or miniature scale. While skilled and attractive work can certainly be accomplished on a larger scale, the miniature is particularly suitable for the aspiring arranger, or anyone who does not have easy access to a garden or a regular supply of freshly picked flowers.

As a city dweller, my initial interest in pressed flower arranging faded when I was confronted by the difficulties of obtaining many of the flowers used in standard arrangements, or in the selection of cultivated varieties recommended by authors. As a result I dismissed the pressed flower medium from my mind as the perogative of the country dweller or of those fortunate enough to possess a town garden. This feeling only vanished as I grew aware of the extraordinary range of plant life which flourishes in urban areas – the curious cosmopolitan garden which flowers on derelict sites awaiting development, or around the borders of temporary car parks, along railway and canal banks, by neglected walls, fences and railings, between paving slabs and in cracks in concrete and in the grassed areas of community lawns, parks, playing grounds, sports fields and road verges.

Conventional arrangements are often restricted to a familiar range of flowers. The miniature, however, draws attention to the tiny plants which often lie unnoticed, precisely because of their diminutive size, while the search for suitable material can produce for all of us a fresh awareness of our everyday surroundings. Placed within a small area, for example, the little Scarlet Pimpernel suddenly acquires a new dimension and, from a miniaturist's viewpoint, a tangle of weeds is transformed into a field of colourful flowers. Tiny plant particles, easily overlooked when included in a large arrangement, provide significant details in the miniature and for the collector. A seeded Shepherd's Purse with glistening pods, for instance, can produce as much pleasure as the sighting of a rare breed of Orchid.

Plants which look large or ungainly at first glance will frequently yield an intriguing crop of bracts, calyxes, stigmas, sepals, stamens and pods when examined more closely and gently taken apart – although it may be necessary to wait for the flowers and leaves to wither away before these shapes stand out clearly and acquire their subtle colouring.

When ripe, the Common Sorrel, which grows on waste land, bears a brilliant galaxy of rust-red stars and once these magnificent fruits have been harvested, a previously derelict stretch becomes an exciting hunting ground as the search continues for similar surprises. The Red Valerian, which blazes on railway embankments, supports fire pink flowers on tough, thick branches which are impossible to press in complete form; only by breaking the branches into small segments can you obtain the slender purple flutes which emerge when dry from the press. The Red Clover, which grows in grass verges, is another plant whose dense clump flower heads seem designed to mislead the collector intent on small specimens – by splitting open the head with a thumbnail, you will find many tiny flowers curving from a stalk in the centre. This is only one example of an unlikely pressing flower which consists of tiny florets or corollas grouped tightly together, each one forming an ideal piece of miniature material when used individually.

On a regular routine walk through a built-up district it is easy for us to overlook the plant life which dwells in brick and stone crevices. Yet near to gutter pipes and gargoyles there are often clusters of ferns and moss mounds and often, slightly above eye-level, there are trails of Ivy and clumps of Ivy-leaved Toadflax with coiling stems and pale violet flowers. At ground level Red Deadnettles sprout between paving cracks; and if you pick one of these street weeds and examine it, you will find soft pink trumpet flowers concealed between downy, heart-shaped leaves.

Weaving through railings and fences are many straggling strands of Cleavers or Goosegrass which divide into distinctive dark stars and the variety of grasses which form elegant sprays when bleached by the sun. By looking with a fresh, enquiring eye at plants or weeds which are usually dismissed as commonplace, the miniaturist will discover a wealth of unusual material to be collected and, in return for a small amount of time taken in exploring an alternative route or walking through an unfamiliar area, there is the prospect of being repaid with the occasional rarity.

While modern development is responsible for levelling large areas of urban land which were once occupied by tenants who took pride in their small back gardens and courtyard flower beds, traces of these buried gardens often survive and can be seen forcing their way through the surface of car parks regardless of the heavy trampling and traffic. In compensation, the motorist often contributes to collections by carrying seeds – caught in clothes, hair, and soles of shoes and the striations of tyres – over considerable distances. Eventually shaken free, these seeds can take root in districts far removed from their original habitat. In dockside and railway areas in fact, it is possible to find plants which have travelled from foreign lands.

From my personal point of view, it is this fascinating

search for natural material that thrives amidst indifference and neglect, and the continual promise of unexpected discoveries, which turns the miniature into the most rewarding form of floral art.

Because of the small scale, the collector will find a wide selection of material more useful than large quantities, and this can be gathered during the year whenever circumstances are suitable. For the arranger with limited leisure, the miniature will prove to be a particularly convenient form of presentation because only a few pieces are required to assemble a simple arrangement and this can be completed within a comparatively short space of time.

This book is designed to introduce the beginner to plant pressing and its potential uses, but I hope it will also persuade any disheartened student to return to an absorbing occupation with a renewed enthusiasm. For the expert, who already has a sound knowledge of pressed material, miniature work might well prove to be a refreshing change from the usual presentations, while some of the small-scale suggestions can be adapted to suit other scales and make use of material which is already in store.

Pressing materials

Plants are preserved by the extraction of their natural moisture. With pressed plants, this can be done by placing freshly picked specimens between sheets of absorbent paper and then storing them under weight or pressure in dry conditions for several weeks. To retain their natural shape during the drying-out period, an even distribution of weight is important.

Book presses

This can be obtained with books, preferably ones of matching size. Old encyclopedias are perfect for this purpose and a full set is a valuable aid for the flower enthusiast! A local auction could produce a mixed assortment of books from a household, including large single volumes and books printed on matt paper. These later are always useful, regardless of size, because the absorbent paper assists the drying. Valued or valuable books should never, however, be used for plant pressing because the extra sheets of inserted storage papers will eventually weaken the spine and distort the book's shape.

Once the papers and material are placed in storage, they should remain undisturbed for a minimum period of six weeks.

Depending on depth, several sets of plant material can be stored in one book, providing sufficient pages are left between each set to leave a smooth, level surface; but it is important not to overload a book to the extent that the cover cannot lie flat or the sets slope towards the centre. Apart from damaging the spine, there is the risk of the material slipping out of position. Also it is difficult to stack other books safely on top.

Cardboard presses

Books can also form the top and base of a flower press when layers of material are placed between the closed covers. A multi-layered press can be easily assembled by cutting sheets of corrugated cardboard to match the size of the book covers. You will need two sheets of card for each set of storage papers. Place one sheet of card on top of the closed base book and, if necessary, place two or three sheets of paper over the card to cover any irregularities in the surface. Place the first set of storage sheets in position, cover with more sheets of paper and then place another two layers of card on top, taking care to keep the edges level. This stacking can be repeated so long as the pile maintains a balanced height. It is then weighted with two or three large volumes. The little tunnels in the corrugated card allow warm air to circulate through the press to speed up the drying.

If the available supply of books has been exhausted, there are other paper sources to consider. Thick disused telephone directories, mail order catalogues, magazines and newspapers can be used but it is important to flank them with firm covers. Thick paperbacks can curl at the edges, while unsupported stacks of glossy paper have a tendency to spill on to the floor. Pieces of plywood make suitable covers and inserts of corrugated card will ventilate the paper bulk. Bricks can be used as weights in place of books but they also should be evenly distributed over the surface of the top cover. With experience, collectors can devise their own version of the flower press and improvisations ranging from converted trouser presses to slats bound with rubber bands

A dark background highlights the finest details, not always to the best advantage! In this arrangement on black velvet, the colours and delicate shapes of the petals, dried seed pods and a bleached Pea tendril are seen clearly whilst the tiny insect bites in the yellow Potentilla flower are also visible.

have all been found serviceable. All types of adaptations can prove successful in fact, providing the following principles of plant pressing are taken into account.

Pressing principles

1. It is essential to use *dry* pressing materials. All books, bricks, corrugated cardboard, papers, wood and printed matter should therefore be thoroughly aired in a warm dry atmosphere well before they are required for pressing. Warm kitchens exposed to clouds of steam should be avoided along with other potentially damp quarters! As a precaution, it is worthwhile running a dry iron over all the paper material to eliminate any trace of moisture which might have accumulated during storage.

2. Plants must be free of external moisture when they are picked for the press. This means that they cannot be collected on wet days or while dew is still on the ground. The safest collecting time is from midday to the afternoon on dry days, although this can be extended on fine summer days. Certain species of plant only thrive in damp, shady surroundings and these will wilt rapidly once they are removed from their habitat.

3. Once a plant is picked, the dying process begins. If much of the original colour and shape is to be preserved therefore, it should be prepared and pressed immediately. Of course, this is not always possible and specimens will require careful packaging if they are to withstand a long journey.

When you are gathering some distance from home, assemble a kit consisting of a suitable carrier, a selection of containers packed with soaked cotton wool or thick domestic tissue, a plastic container of water with a screw stopper and a pair of scissors. Cut the stems close to the ground and group them in the containers according to size. Use the water to refresh the padding from time to time, taking care not to splash the plants. Once home, they can be left to stand in water in a cool area before being prepared for the press.

4. Unless special textures are required, only a smooth surface will produce flowers and leaves fine enough to be included in an arrangement. All pressing papers which cannot be smoothed with a dry iron should be discarded, along with any cracked or damaged corrugated cardboard, for irregularities in the pressing surfaces will in time form indentations on the plant material.

5. If a press is insufficiently weighted, petals and leaves will shrivel up, while uneven weights will produce similarly unwelcome results. While matching bricks or books can be regarded as safe, household objects such as flatirons should be treated with caution. One placed on top of a small pile of books might work effectively but two should not be trusted unless they are identical.

6. Once picked, prepared and left in the press, plants should be left in peace but the impatient beginner often cannot resist checking on their progress. Each unnecessary exposure hinders the drying process while the petals can easily be dislodged whenever the covering sheet is removed.

Travelling press

Quite often, it is the gift of a wooden screw press which awakens a person's interest in plant pressing. This type of press has a distinct advantage over heavy books in that it is compact and easy to carry, but it also has certain drawbacks. The pressure is applied through four screws inserted through the corners of the covers and each time fresh material is added, the screws must be loosened and then replaced. This movement can, as I have pointed out, disturb the contents, and there is also the problem of pressure. Flimsy Primrose petals only require light pressure, while plumper flowers like Daisies require greater pressure. Two dissimilar plants can therefore make poor companions when accommodated within one section of a press. One solution lies in picking only one type of flower or leaf to fill the entire press so only one pressure is required. In a climate where unexpected rain may delay a return visit, this can be a successful way of capturing a particular crop which only flourishes for a brief period. An alternative lies in regarding the screw-press as a temporary travelling measure reserved only for transporting material from the growing site to wherever it can be transferred into a more permanent press. Once these mixed assets are understood, the disillusioned beginner can dismiss early dismal results and start again with greater confidence.

Absorbent papers

There are several different choices that can be made of absorbent papers for storage. Blotting paper can be purchased from stationery departments in a variety of shades and, when a book press is being used, it is worth investing in the thickest quality. Sheets measuring about 10½ × 5 inches (260 × 120mm) are a convenient size for medium and large books because the ends will protrude beyond the pages and serve as a marker. Small pieces, on the other hand, in a large book can be difficult to locate. For clarity, I prefer to store brightly coloured material against a white background, and pale or white pieces on a coloured paper, so that any flaws, such as broken edges, will stand out clearly.

To reduce expense, plain lining paper purchased from decorating departments can be used in place of blotting paper and, in emergencies, for example when presented with an unexpected bunch of flowers, plain writing or typing paper can be used for immediate pressing, although it is advisable to transfer the material to a more absorbent paper at the first opportunity. Providing the paper is plain and clean it will be serviceable, but remember, *never* use printed paper. The inks will discolour the material.

Soft domestic tissue is a useful drying agent but the material should not be placed against folds or perforations. With bulky material, tissue can be used as padding between the plants and the papers, and the final results are often worth the extra trouble of cushioning in this manner. Only use plain toilet paper for this purpose, however; thick kitchen tissue is ideal for a further purpose.

Most household tissues have a pattern embossed on the surface. This fact had escaped my notice until one day when I opened a set of Hydrangea florets and found that each petal was stamped with a pattern of tiny dots. These were removed to a press reserved for oddments and I did not bother to look at them until many months later when I was experimenting with figures dressed in period costume. The petals then proved perfect for representing the textured surface of fabric – so that while kitchen paper is totally unsuitable for preserving natural forms, it can be fun to use it for embossing different petal surfaces.

Specimens and sources

My first plant pressings were gathered from a city centre but, in my eagerness to collect as many specimens as possible, I did not make a note of my local discoveries. This resulted in a great deal of frustration when I went in search of further supplies the following year. On a stretch of waste land near a railway station I had come across a small gathering of pink flowers accompanied by magnificent spiked rust leaves, which I subsequently identified as a species of Cranesbill. Although I was familiar with the general layout, I could not locate the exact place again until the crop had almost died away and only a few withered leaves remained. Another misadventure arose with a track of Herb Robert which sprawled along a tarmac path. This time I had no trouble in locating the plants again but I returned too late in the year, by which time the leaves were large and dark, missing the tiny growths with their brilliant pink colours. A textbook on plant life will give you a general guide on where certain species can be found and their flowering periods, but nature does not always follow a strict pattern.

Selecting material

Varying weather conditions can delay or encourage growth in a particular area, and of course, plants in shadowed positions seldom grow at the same pace as their sun-sited companions. In order to pick the earliest growths and smallest specimens while they are still in a suitable condition for pressing, the collector must be prepared to revisit a potential site at regular intervals. Even a delay of a fortnight can deprive you of a favourite selection of material until it reappears the following year. Since I have missed several crops through neglecting to keep a simple record, I strongly advise any collector to take a note of his or her local discoveries, the exact site on which they were found and the date on which they were picked.

Another mistake of mine was failing to keep a scrap book of specimens because, along with the many delights in store for the collector, there are inevitably also a few disappointments. Some flowers do not retain their original colours when dried, particularly the blue range of wild plants. Notable exceptions are Larkspur and Delphinium, both garden flowers which can be regarded as the permanent blues of the floral palette. Reds often acquire a brownish tinge when dried, bright greenery is apt to lose its fresh tint, pinks and purples can fade into muted beiges and grey tones. Orange and yellow flowers usually show the best colour retention and, while some white flowers remain surprisingly fresh, others turn to a dingy shade of brown.

A large Hydrangea petal is trimmed down to form a bowl that contains an assortment of flowers. The rust leaf of a Cut-leaved Cranesbill and a single Forget-me-not head are positioned to hide the straight scissor cut line which could disturb the natural presentation.

Plant material

Pick a flower head and closely examine its construction. Do the petals join into a tube at the base? If so, it will probably be easy to prepare for pressing. Or does the flower head consist of separate petals held together by a calyx or green particles at the base? Gently press into the centre of the flower to see if the petals fold back easily and remain joined to the base. If the flower disintegrates, it will not stand up to the strain of pressing in the open position but it might be suitable for pressing in the sideway position.

Pick another flower head from the same group and gently press the petals together in a closed position. Exert extra pressure on the calyx with a slight pinch. If the petals remain intact, it will be suitable for pressing in the sideway position. Once the potential strength has been assessed, there are other questions to consider. Are the petals thin and open, or fleshy and close together? Petals like those of the Potentilla will press successfully but if moisture seeps out from a fleshy flower when crushed between the fingertips, it may be difficult to dry out. Bluebells fall within this category and while some arrangers recommend cutting bell shapes into two halves to lessen the bulk, the results are inclined to look strained and unnatural. An easier solution lies in pressing more suitable bell shapes like those which flower on the pink and red Heuchera plants. The dried colour of a flower is sometimes difficult to assess in advance but a wilting flower may give an indication of the final result. If some of the petals have wilted in beige or coffee shades, it is unlikely to retain its original colour but if the shape is attractive you might decide the material is worth preserving. The delicate colours of the Pea flowers often fade away completely but the dried creamy white petals can be overlapped to form full multi-layered flower shapes which cannot be obtained by other means.

Sometimes the frailest of petals are accompanied by large lumpy stigmas in the centres and if these cannot be removed, the petals will shrivel up because they cannot lie flat within the press. When placed in the open or sideway position, do pieces protrude which cannot be plucked away? If so, the complete head is unsuitable for pressing and you will need to decide if the petals are worth pressing individually. Finally, are the flowers in healthy condition and do the selected pressing shapes look attractive? If a flower has to be pruned or forced too much out of its natural shape in the attempt to press it, the result may be awkward and far from appealing. Insects can damage fragile petals, flowers can be snagged by brittle neighbours and scorched or bruised by weather conditions. For some curious reason there are certain flower pressers who are under the impression that blemishes will mysteriously vanish within the press while the opposite occurs. A withered petal or tattered edge may escape detection amongst living plants but once pressed, these flaws will stand out clearly. Like ladies who are subject to good and bad days, flowers also have their off-peak periods and there is little point in picking those which are reluctant to come out or who are downright dowdy around the edges. With a little effort beautiful specimens can be sorted from those which are far from perfect and while commercial arrangers often seem content to use material which is second-rate, miniature artists should reserve their skill and patience for the finest materials.

TOP. *An old-fashioned oval brooch is restored with a cream satin lining and a new perspex cover.*

BELOW. *A silk-lined pendant shows a flimsy pink flower firmly secured in the centre with a single Forget-me-not head.*

RIGHT. *Two watch glasses are glued together to make a pendant which contains an arrangement on each side. The work is suspended in a silver mount designed to hold a crown piece.*

LEFT. *A pendant is lined with a piece of shot-silk cut from a Tulip petal.*

Selection list of Miniature material

At present, I have several unfamiliar plants in the process of being pressed and until the time comes to examine them, I will not know whether they have dried successfully. Each year I try to collect large quantities of the material which I know will dry well and prove useful in arrangements, but I also reserve room for a few strangers for experimental purposes. A collector's list of recommended plants must therefore remain incomplete but, for the beginner, here is a short selection of Miniature material and the sources where it can be easily obtained in most areas.

NAME	LOCATION	PART FOR PRESSING
Alyssum	From seed or garden nurseries	Flowers
Aquilegia (Columbine)	Garden nurseries, sometimes wild	Leaves
Broom	Commons, wastelands	Flowers
Buttercup	Grass banks, fields, wastelands	Flowers
Candytuft	From seed	Flowers and leaves
Cleavers (Goosegrass)	Hedges, fences, wastelands	Leaves
Clover	Grass verges, banks	Flowers and leaves
Cow Parsley	Roadsides, ditches, wastelands	Floret clusters
Cowslips (Cultivated)	From seed or garden nurseries	Flowers, calyx, stems
Curly Chevril	Herb bed, garden nurseries	Cream leaves
Cut-leaved Cranesbill	Grass lands, wastelands	Rust, spiked leaves
Daisy (Lawn)	Lawns, grass lands, wastelands	Flowers
Delphinium	Garden nurseries, florist	Florets
Fat Hen Dock	Waysides, wastelands	Flowers
Ferns	Woods, walls, florist	Leaves
Forget-me-not	From seed, garden nurseries, stream banks	Flowers and sprigs
Geums	Garden nurseries	Flowers, rust leaves
Gold Dust	Garden nurseries	Flowers
Gorse	Heaths, wastelands	Flowers
Grasses	Road sides, wastelands	Bleached tips
Ground ivies	Hedges, undergrowth, wastelands	Flowers, small leaves
Heather	Moors, garden nurseries	Flowers
Herb Robert	Hedgerows, verges, tracks	Leaves
Heuchera	Garden nurseries	Flowers
Hop Trefoil	Grass verges, meadows	Flowers and stems
Iberis	From seed, garden nurseries	Flowers
Ivy	Brickwork, woods, florist	Leaves
Ivy-leaved Toadflax	Brick and stonework, walls	Leaves, stems and flowers
Lady's Smock	Meadows	Flowers
Larkspur	From seed, garden nurseries, florist	Florets

NAME	LOCATION	PART FOR PRESSING
Lesser Celandine	Grass banks, roadsides, hedges	Flowers
Lobelia	From seed, garden nurseries	Flowers
Melilot	Wastelands, fields, hedges, seed, garden nurseries	Flowers
Montbretia	Garden nurseries, florist	Flowers
Moss	Brickwork, woods, florist	Strands
Nettles	Roadsides, wastelands	Flowers, small leaves
Pansy (Dwarf)	From seed, garden nurseries	Flowers
Peas	Vegetable plot, grass banks	Tendrils
Periwinkle	From seed, shaded areas, wood banks	Flowers
Polyanthus	From garden nurseries	Flowers, calyx and stems
Potentilla	Shrub, garden nurseries	Flowers and leaves
Primroses	Woodlands, banks, roadsides	Flowers, calyx and stems
Red Valerian	Railway banks, stone walls	Flowers
Rock Roses	Rockery, garden nurseries	Flowers
Rosebay Willowherb	Wastelands, roadsides	Florets
Scarlet Pimpernel	Garden weed, wastelands	Flowers, stems and leaves
Sorrel (Common)	Meadows, wastelands	Flowers
Speedwell	Banks, fields, wastelands	Flowers, stems and leaves
Sweet Peas	From garden nurseries	Flowers and tendrils
Verbena	From garden nurseries	Flowers
Vetch (All varieties)	Grass banks, meadows	Flowers and tendrils
Wild Pansy	Hills, pasture, wastelands	Flowers

If you extend your search into the countryside for wild plants, it is important to remember that some species are in danger of becoming extinct. It is also illegal to uproot any wild plant without the landowner's consent and because it is essential that flowers should be left to seed if they are to survive, I have recommended cultivated Cowslips from a nursery instead of the wild variety. Packets of wild plant seed can now be purchased and these should be sown and raised whenever possible in order to conserve our countryside. Because you will only need small quantities of flowers, there is little harm in picking a few Primroses; but never remove all the flower heads from one plant because it is this form of careless collecting which will in time eliminate an entire species.

Leaves, stems and tendrils

With a beautiful selection of colourful flowers demanding our immediate attention, it is easy to overlook the important role played in arrangements by leaves and stems.

Very often, the flower head will form the main focal point of colour but leaves and stems add the delicate balance and movement to a design. For each flower you may need two or three leaves, so press a wide selection in sufficient quantities. Curling stems are particularly useful; these should also be collected in large numbers, along with other coiling and curving shapes.

Preparing plants for the press

At one time or another, you might have casually picked and pressed a flower inside a book only to have forgotten about it until a much later date. If the result was a smooth, well-defined specimen, luck probably played a large part because most unprepared pressings emerge in confused clumps of unrecognizable plant matter. This is caused through the different thicknesses contained in various parts of one plant. In order to obtain flowers and leaves suitable for arrangements, it is necessary to separate the plants into sections and eliminate surplus bulk wherever possible. With the exception of very small plants like Scarlet Pimpernel or Speedwell, the stalks should be removed from flower heads and the temptation to press a mixed selection together should always be resisted because the slightest variation in thickness will greatly increase the risk of distortion through shrinkage and shrivelling. In many instances, only one part of a plant is required and to avoid wasting valuable storage space, it is sensible to prepare sufficient material to cover one sheet of storage paper.

As your collection increases, you will notice several basic variations in flower head construction and the following guide will help you to prepare some of the main types in a suitable manner.

Cups and saucers (Figs. 1, 1a)

Primroses along with many other saucer-shaped flowers have petals which join into a tube at the base. To enable a head to open out flat, it is necessary to remove the tube by snipping it away with a small pair of sharp scissors. Although hardly visible at the time, petals can be bruised by heavy handling so, whenever possible, hold a plant by the stem with the head facing downwards over the sheet of paper selected for storage. If possible, trim so that the head falls directly on to the sheet facing downwards.

fig. 1

fig. 1a

When a sufficient quantity has been prepared, space them apart with a needle inserted through the small hole in the centre. Flower petals should never overlap, and because they will take up more space when pressed flat it is worth leaving a little more space between them than seems strictly necessary.

When pressing cup or saucer shapes in the sideway position, leave the tube in place. These can be trimmed away once the flower has dried. Some arrangers use a two-thirds position by placing a head in the sideway position and then folding back a portion of the upper petals, but the straight line which is folded through the centre is inclined to look unnatural, especially on larger flowers.

Flutes and trumpets (Figs. 2, 2a, 3, 3a)

Nettles, Ground Ivies and some species of wild Orchid have tubular-based trumpet flowers which can be coaxed from their bracts by careful handling. When pressed sideways, the fluted lips will form elegant trumpet shapes but, when pressed facing upwards, they are inclined to look squat and somewhat squashed. Small shapes like these should be arranged in rows facing in one direction with the top of the

fig. 2

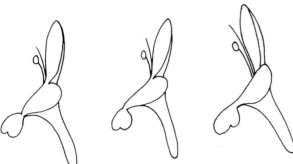

fig. 2a

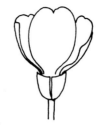

fig. 3a

flowers pointing towards the upper edge of the storage sheet. The covering sheet can then be applied so that it rolls from the base to the top of the petals, helping to smooth out potential puckers and creases. The same layout should be used for rows of single petals, for flowers with separated petals placed in the sideway position, and for leaves.

fig. 3

In their original condition, some of the flowers shown in these small pendants would have been too large or too poor in quality for miniature presentation. Careful plucking can extend the range of material or display it in a different manner.

Top. *A yellow spray is completed with two single Melilot florets taken from the top of the flower head.*

Right. *The shrivelled petals of a poorly pressed Buttercup are removed to reveal the bright stamens in the centre.*

Left. *The outer petals of a pink Candytuft are picked out to leave a small, well-defined flower head.*

Pot bellies (Figs. 4, 4a)

The Common Lawn Daisy with its plump raised centre often looks disappointingly straggly when pressed, but when it is treated with a very firm hand, it responds surprisingly well.

Because Daisies grow in great abundance, it is easy to pick too many at one time and, quite often, too little attention is given to the condition of the flower. Do not be fooled into thinking that one Daisy is very much the same as the next because, if you look closely, you will find some which look full and firm while others appear to have been on a diet.

Only pick a few of the plumpest ones, remove the stalks and place them face downwards on the paper. Press down each base very firmly with the thumb to flatten out the centres, cover as quickly as possible and store under extra heavy weight, such as under a pile of books. The Buttercup with its bulbous centre should also be treated in the same heavy-handed manner because the petals will swiftly shrivel up if prepared in a timid fashion.

fig. 4a

fig. 4

The natural curves in this arrangement are supplied by the Scarlet Pimpernel stems, slyly extended with a tip of fern leaf and a spray of Fennel, a coiling tendril and a small sprig of Forget-me-not. The pale blue curve just above the pale green strand of moss is slightly suspect for, to balance the blues, it was sliced from a Delphinium petal.

Other dubious shapes include the single pink petal added to strengthen the colour of the Scarlet Pimpernels along with an Alyssum floret, while a pink Candytuft floret plucked from the main head serves the same purpose on the lower right-hand side. Beyond all belief, there is the pink and yellow flower which was manufactured to extend the pink tones and the yellow florets of Gold Dust. Unlike the naturalist restricted to accurate detail, the miniaturist is free to choose, cut, and compile whenever necessary. And cheat!

Bush heads   (Figs. 5, 5a)

Some flowers, like Alyssum or Gold Dust, have a bushy head which extends down the stalk with growth and do not have a distinctive part, such as a bract, to serve as a cutting guide. These should be held head downwards above the paper and snipped across the stem just below the fullest spread of petals or before the petals start to thin out. With pyramid shapes, snip off the points and press these together in one set of paper. Trim the remaining lengths of stalks with petals into thin slices to use as flower wheels or particles.

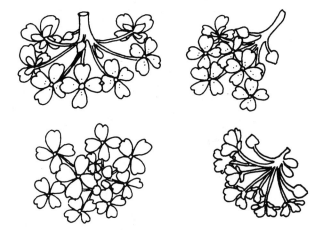

fig. 5a

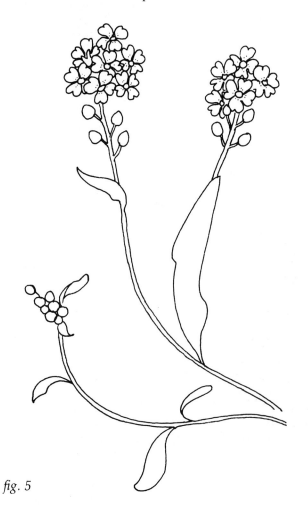

fig. 5

TOP LEFT. *The lower tip of a Daisy spray is finished with bleached grass and a seed pod with two Candytuft florets.*

TOP CENTRE. *A circular spray is completed with single Cow Parsley florets falling from a pink Nettle flute.*

TOP RIGHT. *A rust and yellow arrangement with a curved piece of trimmed ribbon cut from a Carnation petal.*

BELOW LEFT. *Two Vetch flowers and a yellow Melilot tip curve towards an Aquilegia leaf.*

BELOW CENTRE. *Bleached colours and dried heads with a soft golden centre of Broom flowers.*

BELOW RIGHT. *A pink Larkspur flower trimmed to look in one direction faces towards the centre of the frame, not away from the edge.*

22

23

Clusters (Figs. 6, 6a)

Various types of hedgerow parsley thrive on the roadside. From a distant glance, it is difficult to distinguish them from Wild Carrot and Hemlock because they all bear clusters of white florets.

Cow Parsley, often called Queen Anne's Lace, is a suitable pressing variety because the thin bracteoles at the base of each cluster easily open out and allow the florets to lie flat. Cut the smallest clusters from their stalks just below the bracteoles and arrange them facing downwards on the paper. Before covering, press down each base in order to spread the florets to their fullest extent because these clusters can take up a surprising amount of space.

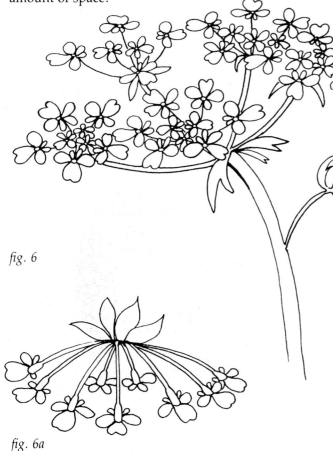

fig. 6

fig. 6a

Once familiar with miniature work, the tiny size of these pots and pill containers will provide an amusing challenge for the arranger.

TOP RIGHT. *A Potentilla flower on a blue Delphinium base is surrounded with pink Alyssum florets.*

BOTTOM RIGHT. *A garland arrangement surrounds a Cranesbill leaf.*

CENTRE. *Scarlet Pimpernels spray from a trimmed rust leaf.*

TOP LEFT. *Small, smaller and the smallest Forget-me-not heads!*

BOTTOM LEFT. *The lower tip of the spray is completed with a single star of Common Sorrel. The upper tip is finished with a fragment of grass, Curly Chevril and a dried Shepherd's Purse pod.*

24

Multi-layers (*Figs. 7, 7a*)

Flowers which have several layers of petals can be successfully pressed, although their bulk will have to be lessened by plucking out some of the petals. This requires a certain amount of skill and judgement because, if too many petals are removed, the head will disintegrate into a shower of separate petals. After varying results, I now prefer to remove only the minimum number of petals before pressing under extra weight, and I leave the final trimming until the material has dried out. Creased petals can be removed from the front and the shape is often more delicate and clearly defined after the larger petals have been plucked from the back.

Although curly and full, the double florets of Delphiniums dry surprisingly well. Snip the florets from the stalk and arrange facing downwards, pressing down the protruding spurs with your fingertip before covering. A full floret is often too large for a small arrangement but one will supply many lovely petals which can be used individually and it is worth searching for the Black Eye varieties which are extremely beautiful. The Larkspur can also be prepared in the same manner.

fig. 7

Singles and sprays (*Figs. 8, 8a*)

Some plants have flowers which are suitable for pressing in spray form, or individually; and one of the best examples is the Forget-me-not with its tiny saucer-shaped flowers and curving branches. Although the handling of petals is best generally avoided, a slight squeeze on some of the partially opened buds will help to define the pressing shape. Position the sprigs with the fully opened flowers facing upwards and the buds resting sideways. Even when these pressings are not entirely successful, the small curls of closed buds can be retained for detail. Fully opened flower heads can be snipped directly on to the storage sheet of paper and separated into place with a needle.

fig. 7a

Because these little flowers are so suitable for miniature work, it is worth preparing them in large quantities. By placing the plants in water on a sunny window ledge after the first crop of opened heads has been gathered, the buds will open out to provide further supplies. Speedwell and Scarlet Pimpernel are also two-way pressers but because their petals are so flimsy, they are easier to press sideways.

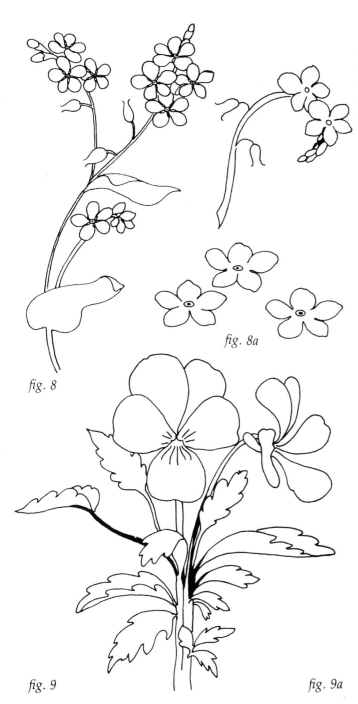

fig. 8a

fig. 8

fig. 9

Curlers (Figs. 9, 9a)

Dwarf Pansies, and members of the Viola family, can be difficult to control because their petals have a tendency to curl up as soon as they are picked. Only pick a few at one time, therefore, and leave a small length of stalk attached to each head because the irregular petals will fall apart if trimmed too closely.

Place them facing downwards with the larger upper petals pointing towards the top of the storage sheet. Press down the protruding spurs with the fingertip and roll the covering sheet first into position over the lower petals. If this is done speedily, these elusive flower faces can be successfully captured.

The bright Rosebay Willowherb is also inclined to droop within minutes of picking and one plant with several open florets is usually ample for one pressing. Cut the florets beneath the purple pointed base and arrange face downwards on the paper. Even when the petals fail to press well, the dark sepals provide interesting shapes.

fig. 9a

Spikes and spears (Figs. 10, 10a)

Tall, spikey plants like Common Sorrel and Melilot should be cut into strands of convenient length for the press and if they are stiff and bulky, they should be padded with layers of thin absorbent tissue. The tips with the smallest flowers can be used in arrangements while the lengths with the blunt cut tips are only suitable for supplying particles.

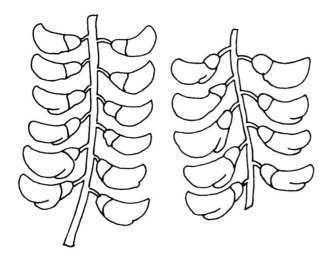

fig. 10

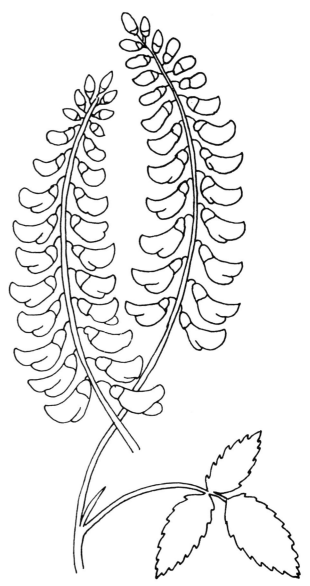

fig. 10a

TOP LEFT. *Small tips of fern do not distract from these well preserved Buttercups.*

TOP CENTRE. *Three tiny clover leaves tumble towards Scarlet Pimpernels.*

TOP RIGHT. *Curling Delphinium petals add width and colour into a thin spray of fragments.*

BELOW LEFT. *The lower half of a circular spray is completed with three strands of Red Valerian.*

BELOW CENTRE. *A bright red Rose petal bowl bulges with flowers.*

BELOW RIGHT. *A butterfly descends on pink Orchid.*

Fat heads (Figs. 11, 11a)

Thick Clover heads should be split into segments and pressed under extra weight while the smaller clover shaped flowers like the yellow Hop Trefoil and Black Medick can be pressed complete with a short amount of stalk.

Preparing the plants

Before preparing the plants, place the lower sheet of blotting paper on the page of the opened book in which it is to be stored or on the cardboard sheet of a multi-layered press. This will prevent unnecessary movement of the material afterwards. When the plant pieces have been prepared and spaced apart correctly, the upper sheet should be lowered into position very slowly because swift movement can disturb all your careful preparation.

On a strip of paper, clearly mark the name of the stored pieces and the date on which they were pressed. Place this beside the set so that the information protrudes from the page. Sometimes, when I was in a hurry, I neglected to do this at the time with the intention of marking the contents later. It is a mistake, especially when using encyclopaedias matching in shape, size and colour, and for the saved two or three minutes I have in the long run wasted hours.

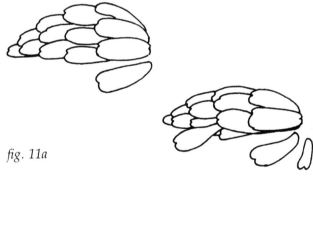

fig. 11a

fig. 11

An arrangement containing a white Iberis flower, flanked with leaves of sun-bleached Fool's Parsley and green Aquiligea leaves, receives extra emphasis in a mounted presentation.

Arrangements

Assembling dried material

While some people seem to possess a natural talent for artistic arrangements, others have to acquire the skill by simple stages. Achieving a graceful design with dried plant material often requires a certain amount of practice, especially when working for the first time on a small scale. To avoid spoiling good miniature bases with early experiments, mark out the shape and size of the base several times on scrap paper and when a frame is to be added, clearly mark where the inner edge of the frame will lie inside the base. This will give an accurate idea of the available space because it is easy to over-estimate the size of the working surface.

Select various pieces of dried material and place them inside the marked areas in order to gain a correct idea of their size. Very often, a small leaf or flower will seem surprisingly large when first encircled within the miniature area.

These abstract compositions consist of overlapping petals which allow the underlying colours and shapes to merge into subtle shades. Apart from making good use of petals which are generally·unsuitable – because they are too large, misshapen, flimsy or faded – they also offer a different form of art work. Success depends on the swirling balance of colour and the floating impression of petals.

LEFT. *Yellow Carnation petals lap against the black-tipped petals of Delphinium.*

RIGHT. *Pink Geranium petals in fanned and folded positions form orange tones over a yellow Primrose base. Overlaid Delphiniums produce shades of slate-blue with a Candytuft floret supplying the splash of bright pink.*

Individual pieces of material can be transported on a needle steadied with the index finger; the tweezers used by many arrangers are often too large for the little pieces although they can be used for handling larger shapes. Continue to experiment with different pieces of plant matter until you become familiar with the shapes, sizes and the surrounding space. A successful arrangement should be neatly contained within the framed area, with sufficient space to show detail to the best advantage. A common mistake is over-crowding, with too many pieces, or making the arrangement too large, resulting in visual confusion or ugly broken blunt edges when the arrangement is cut off by the frame.

Whenever possible, always aim for uniform thickness in dried material, particularly when using plastic film as a covering. Thin petals can be overlapped or superimposed, but frail material should never be placed over bulky pieces, such as a stiff stalk, because it will crack or crease when the protective covering is eventually pressed firmly into place. Stalks and leaves can be trimmed at the base with scissors to meet the edge of delicate petals; a tapered or diagonal cut will look more elegant than a blunt straight snip.

Plant material can be secured into position with light applications of adhesive suitable for paper, and this can be purchased in tube or pencil form from stationery departments. Once fixed, dried material should not be moved; brittle pieces are liable to snap and exposed spots of adhesive will discolour in time. Always arrange the main pieces in a harmonious, basic design prior to fixing so that the shapes and colours can be adjusted when necessary. If a piece of fixed material must be removed, lift it up with a needle and scrape away all trace of the adhesive with a fine point. A paper surface will probably show scratch marks but these can often be disguised by covering with another piece of material.

Adhesive techniques

Depending on the size and shape to be secured, adhesive can be applied in two ways. With a larger piece, such as a fully opened flower head or leaf, a speck of adhesive can be removed directly from the container with the point of a needle and lightly spread on to the surface of the background. The piece can then be placed on top and lightly pressed down with the fingertip. If the piece is very tiny, lift it up on a needle point and place a minute speck underneath it before positioning it in the arrangement. After a certain amount of practice, you will learn where to place adhesive specks so they cannot be seen, or, alternatively, how to disguise them. A group of slender particles, such as a stemmed Scarlet Pimpernel, a strand of moss and a seed pod can be secured at their bases with one speck of adhesive which can then be covered by a tiny flower like a single Forget-me-not head. Whenever possible, avoid spreading adhesive under stems or flower heads if they can be secured at the base because they will lie in a more natural position when fixed in this manner.

During the early stages, the beginner may frequently be faced with the problem of applying adhesive too scantily, so that the arrangement easily becomes dislodged, or of applying too much so that it seeps out on the base when the material is pressed into place. Certain types of adhesive also become thick and lumpy when exposed to the atmosphere for a time: these should be discarded because the adhesive cannot be spread smoothly and the bumps will become apparent under flimsy material. A few trial runs with some inferior specimens on scrap paper will help you to become familiar with the fixing technique. It will also save a great deal of irritation when it comes to assembling your first miniatures.

Working conditions

If there happens to be a spare room available for your assembling sessions, book it and hang a bold "Keep Out" sign outside the door because there are few occupations more precarious than handling feather light pieces of dried material. Once you start work, it will be necessary to uncover several sheets of stored material in order to select suitable shapes and colours and the slightest rush of air – from a sudden movement to a small sneeze – will be sufficient to scatter your specimens all over the place. A swiftly opened door will have the force of a hurricane and a gust of breeze through a window will assume gale strength. If an invasion of the workroom is unavoidable, insist that all who enter approach with the speed of a weary snail. Even in isolation, however, your material might not be safe. An unexpected cough has scattered an arrangement which has taken me hours to prepare and carefully positioned particles have been brushed out of place when I have forgotten to pin back my hair.

Whenever possible, work on a large table in front of a closed window by natural daylight or use an adjustable angle lamp for extra light. In deep concentration it is easy to continue working without noticing the change of light and it is a mistake to work in the shadows cast by your hands or shoulders. Work which looks competent in such conditions often looks shoddy when reviewed in daylight.

Because the time factor cannot be completely ignored when working with exposed dried material, I like to prepare with a full pack of needles and a pin cushion, two sources of adhesive, a saucer and a couple of pairs of small scissors so that time is not wasted by searching. Neat workers will probably manage to wipe needles clear of adhesive with a sheet of tissue, but for the less methodical I recommend a piece of old sheeting to be

Warm rusts contrast against cool creams on a dark brown background to create a suggestion of autumn. The tips of bleached grass form the main lines of the sweeping spray and, to continue the circular shape, Heuchera flowers have been spaced around the base below the Iberis flower.

Subdued tones can often be enhanced with sparing touches of bright colour.

used as a cover over the working surface. All blobs of adhesive can be wiped on to the edge and you will have the advantage of knowing exactly where they are. Tacky tissue can easily catch on clothing and, once the adhesive smears, it is not difficult to emerge after a session with a fancy outfit decked with stray petals!

Whenever possible, aim to complete one miniature during one session, including the sealing and framing, because the material cannot be left uncovered especially in a room which is only used occasionally. It will soon become limp and useless or curl up around the edges. Dried material should be stored in conditions similiar to those used for pressing: a stack with inserted sheets of corrugated cardboard is a convenient method. It is inadvisable to store pieces in envelopes because the brittle material will snap into fragments should they rub together. After a while, you will amass an assortment of particles, loose petals and oddments and these should be stored together in a set and clearly marked. This mixed pack will prove extremely useful when searching for tiny finishing touches with which to complete an arrangement.

A selection of arrangements

Until you become accustomed to handling material with confidence, it is best to restrict your first arrangements to a few well-chosen pieces. Once the various methods of securing the pieces have been mastered, you will be able to create an infinite variety of original work. The following arrangements are just a few suggestions from the potential range.

Leaf swags   (Figs. 12, 12a, 12b)

Providing each thickness is correctly positioned, leaves can be overlapped into graceful swags to form an elegant base for flower heads. To make a simple swag, select one well-defined leaf with a straight central vein, like an Ivy, and two curving leaves. When using two leaves which point in the same direction it might be necessary to turn one upside down in order to continue

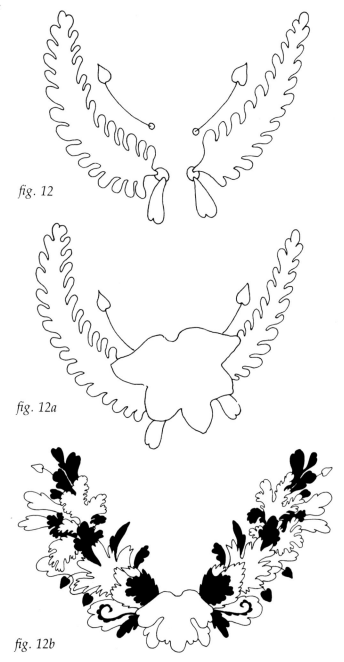

fig. 12

fig. 12a

fig. 12b

the line of the curve. Space the two curved leaves slightly apart to form an arc, and place the straight leaf in the centre so that it just covers the bottoms of the leaves. Adjust the leaves until they form a balanced swag, then carefully remove the central leaf so the outer leaves can be secured at their bases with adhesive. Replace the central leaf and secure with adhesive.

Longer and more elaborate swags can be assembled with the addition of more curving leaves but always position the frailest varieties at the outer tips and over-lap towards the centre with firmer specimens. Details like Pea tendrils, seed pods, Nettle, and Clover flowers or moss strands can be worked into these arrangements, but care should be taken not to place them too close to the outer edge of the base because these may be stretched slightly out of position when the miniature is covered and framed.

Flower borders (Figs. 13, 13a)

Delicate borders of flowers, leaves and particles, which consist of small separate groups, will form an attractive arrangement and, at the same time, will teach you the basic technique of assembling plant material and how to hide the adhesive successfully. In Figure 13 the finer details are fixed into place with specks of adhesive. When securing a fully opened flower head, place the adhesive on the spot where the centre of the flower will rest or, if a centre has been removed, place the adhesive near the opening.

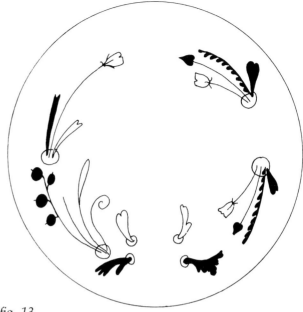

fig. 13

fig. 13a

37

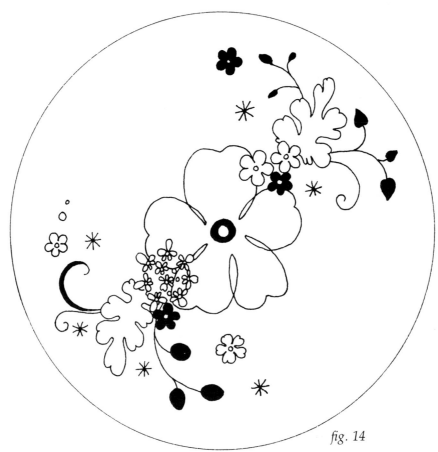

fig. 14

Single spray (Fig. 14)

A single well-defined flower head can form the centre piece of a simple arrangement and, because this basic composition will draw attention to the finest detail, it is worth selecting a perfectly preserved specimen for such a prominent position. The tiny sprays which flank a central flower head often look more graceful if they are arranged in a curving diagonal direction instead of a straight-across line and the gaps between flower and sprays can be filled with smaller flower heads. The tiny clusters of florets such as Cow Parsley, Alyssum and Gold Dust make very useful filling material because they link an arrangement together without disturbing the colour balance with too much density.

A mauve Pansy changes her original complexion for a flattering colour of palest cream!

Against a white background, this subtle transformation would be lost while the colour balance could also be disturbed with the eventual loss of the central tint. When working with fast faders, use a contrasting background so that the shapes can be fully appreciated long after the colours have departed. In anticipation of the change of colour, a light Curly Chervil leaf has been positioned to extend the Pansy shape towards the base.

38

Frames and fittings

If pressed flower work is to survive for any length of time it must be preserved in sealed, airtight conditions. While this inevitably excludes some forms of presentation there is still a wide selection available providing the correct measures are taken.

Wooden frames and suitable mounts

Conventional frames can be used but wooden ones must be carefully checked for dust. When the frame is wiped clean, sharply tap each side to see if it sheds sawdust or dirt. If the frame is sound but continues to shed particles, bind the raw edges with strips of gummed paper tape. Should the wood prove wormed or warped, discard it.

It is essential that the glass fits exactly into the front of the frame. To prevent your work from becoming damp or damaged in a frame-maker's workshop, it is best to buy the glass from the framer or a glazier before the arrangement has been assembled. Once you have all the frame fittings, the work can be fitted and sealed immediately on completion. A new frame is usually supplied with a backing board but, with an old frame, it may be necessary to have a piece of hardboard cut to fit into the back. Cardboard is not strong enough to use as a backing board but, to create a snug fit, you will probably need to insert sheets of cardboard between the arrangement and the backing board. These should be exactly the same size as the backing board, not slightly smaller because air pockets will form in the corners. Apply card to a level so that when the backing board is placed in position it rests slightly above the back of the frame, not sunken below it – because this will leave a slight gap which will eventually allow moisture inside. All metal clips and screws should be removed from the back of the frame and when the glass, arrangement, cards and backing have been layered, the edges should be sealed with strips of gummed paper.

Because of the sealed factor, a thick card mount should *never* be used with pressed flowers. The petals will soon curl up and the arrangement swiftly deteriorate. Thin paper mounts can be used with arrangements but, because of the difficulty of cutting paper into smooth shapes, it is best to purchase these from a professional source. Glass printed with mount shapes can also be purchased and these provide a satisfactory and pleasing style of presentation.

An alternative method lies in assembling the arrangement on a base smaller than the area to be framed and placing a piece of coloured card, or card covered with fabric behind it so the work is surrounded with a coloured border.

When mounting a picture in this manner, select the coloured card to fit snugly inside the frame. If fabric is being used, fold the edges back firmly and stitch them together with thread across the back of the card. Assemble the arrangement on a piece of professionally cut paper or thin card with the correct dimensions – because it is very difficult to correct the size of an arrangement afterwards with scissors. The edges of the paper will be clearly on display and if these look tatty or out of line, it will spoil the presentation.

A small porcelain frame holds an arrangement on blue satin. Because the inside of the frame is slightly irregular and cannot be fitted tightly with glass, the work is protected with self-adhesive film. The base is padded to hold the work in place and the back is sealed with thick card glued to the edge of the frame.

41

Locked frames and fabric backgrounds

Many of the miniatures in this book are assembled in locked frames which are manufactured for pressed-flower work and range from one inch to six inches in size. The frames can be purchased complete with a perspex covering, a card base, a layer of thin foam padding to place behind the base, a locking plate and a backing card, along with instructions for assembling them correctly. Coloured card can be used in place of the plain card provided, or you may prefer to use an attractive scrap of fabric as an alternative background. From a large scrap bag collected for the purpose, I have experimented with silks, crepe-de-chine, satins and velvets in a wide assortment of colours to show certain flowers to the best advantage. Other fabrics can be used, but it is best to avoid pronounced textures and tones which might distract from the natural shades of the dried material. Always iron the fabric first and if steam has to be used to remove stubborn creases, leave the fabric to air overnight in a warm place. Velvet should also be dry-ironed on the back to make the pile more manageable.

Remove the perspex, foam, plate and backing card to one side and cut a square of fabric large enough to cover the base card with a generous allowance all round. Fit the frame into place over the fabric and card, adjusting the fabric until it lies smooth and flat in the manner used for fastening material into a needlework ring. With the frame still in position, assemble the flower arrangement and remove the frame when the work is completed. The arrangement should then be covered by the perspex, but remember, this is a tricky stage as loose petals and particles can easily lift up through static and catch on to the cover. I have found that by wiping the perspex clean with a natural, not synthetic, piece of rag and then rubbing it lightly across my cheek, the material is more inclined to remain in position.

When the perspex is in place, replace the frame and insert the piece of foam behind the base card beneath the folds of the fabric. Trim away the surplus fabric and then press the locking plate into position. If thick velvet has been used, this might be difficult and it will be necessary to remove the frame to trim the fabric away exactly around the edge of the base card. If possible, hold the perspex in position while trimming and blow away the cut threads while you work because these can easily slip into the flower arrangement and can be very tedious to remove with a needle point. A small piece of self-adhesive tape or film rolled into a circle will be useful for picking up loose specks from a background but do not touch any part of the arrangement because it will also lift this away as well. Once the locking plate is in position, the back card will fit easily into place.

Assembling a velvet mount

Apart from frames, there are other items manufactured with mounts for miniature decoration and these include pendants for jewellery which can be threaded on chains or fixed to brooch fittings, pill boxes, tiny trinket pots, lidded bowls, compact and key fobs. For an impressive presentation, a miniature can be enclosed in a velvet mount. The arrangement opposite was assembled on a pot lid and fitted into a frame, both purchased from the same source.

A different form of mounted miniature displays a Candytuft flower head flanked with green Geranium leaves, purple Hydrangea flowers and Aquilegia leaves with two tiny Trefoils at the top. Cow Parsley and pink Alyssum clusters break up the strong, dark colours which could easily overpower the soft pink colouring in the centre.

This arrangement is sealed inside a frame and inserted into a padded velvet mount. Instructions for making the mount are given overleaf.

A two-toned dwarf Pansy flower lies between two trumpets of Montbretia. Each trumpet has been carefully trimmed towards the base to eliminate bulk and produce a more graceful shape while the petals remain untouched. The spray is extended with sprigs of Common Sorrel, Heuchera flowers, a faded Hawthorn leaf and Gold Dust fragments. The leaf and florets lift up the light yellow centre of the Pansy which would otherwise be overshadowed by the rich rusts and oranges.

A lively collection of plant life overspills from a Tulip vase. Two slender heads of dried moss spring between the dark green leaves of the Ivy-leaved Toadflax while a cluster of pink Alyssum bursts free from the bunch. A further sense of movement is suggested by placing a few fragments in the downward, falling position with tiny pieces arranged around the base to resemble recently fallen petals.

To make a similar mount, you will need the following items:-

One 4in/10cm lid, complete with locking plate.
One 6in/15cm frame, minus perspex or glass.
One 6in/15cm circle of firm card.
7 square in/18cm of quilt padding.
8 square in/21cm of velvet.
A needle, strong scissors, thread: plus the usual miniature materials with which to arrange the lid.

Use the backing from the frame as a guide for marking the 6in/15cm circle of card and cut just inside the marked line because the velvet will take up space when folded over the edge of the card. Place the velvet square face downwards and put the card in the centre. Mark 1in/2.5cm all around the card circle, using a chalk pencil if the fabric is dark. Cut out the velvet circle. Thread the needle and double knot the end. Pierce through the velvet so the knot lies on the piled surface ¼in/6mm away from the edge of the fabric. Make a circle of small even stitches around the edge and finish with the thread running loosely out next to the knot. Make another row of stitches ¼in/6mm inside the first row in the same manner (see Fig. 15).

Place the circle of card on the padding, mark the edge and cut out a circle of padding to match the card. Remove the padding to one side and fit the card inside the frame. Place the lid in the centre and mark the edge, having measured equal distances from edge to edge so the lid is exactly central. Cut out the centre of the card and fit the lid into the opening. If it fits tightly, enlarge the opening slightly because the velvet will take up room when it is folded back through the opening.

Replace the card on the padding and mark the centre opening; trim the padding to match, and then secure the padding and the card together with adhesive. Trim the edge of the padding at a diagonal angle in order to taper the depth. Place the velvet circle facing pile downwards and position the padded card on top with the padding against the back of the velvet. Slowly draw up the threads and evenly gather in the velvet until it folds back smoothly and firmly around the edge of the card. Secure the gathering with small stitches.

Pierce the centre of the velvet circle with scissor points and cut out a circle ½in/1cm smaller than the centre of the card. Snip into the edge of the circle at regular intervals, cutting just below the edge of the card, to enable the velvet to fold back. Using firmly knotted double thread, catch the two velvet edges together with taut regular oversewing stitches to produce a firm, smooth surface, (see Fig. 16). Secure the thread with stitches, trim away any surplus fabric bulk and fit the padded velvet circle inside the frame. Position the backing card in behind the mount and secure with pins. Apply adhesive in the centre and secure the assembled pot lid inside the mount.

Another presentation can be prepared by simply padding the card as described without removing the centre. The miniature can then be secured to the velvet surface with adhesive, producing a raised centrepiece like the one on page 8.

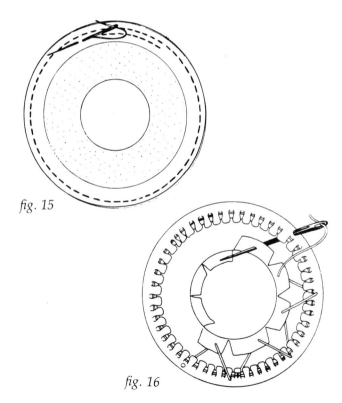

fig. 15

fig. 16

1981 list of protected plants

(under the Wildlife and Countryside Act, 1981)

Adder's-tongue, least *Ophioglossum lusitanicum*
Adder's-tongue, spearwort *Ranunculus ophioglossifolius*
Alison, small *Alyssum alyssoides*
Bladder-fern, Dickie's *Cystopteris dickieana*
Broomrape, bedstraw *Orobanche caryophyllacea*
Broomrape, oxtongue *Orobanche loricata*
Broomrape, thistle *Orobanche reticulata*
Cabbage, Lundy *Rhynchosinapis wrightii*
Calamint, wood *Calamintha sylvatica*
Catchfly, Alpine *Lychnis alpina*
Cinquefoil, rock *Potentilla rupestris*
Club-rush, triangular *Scirpus triquetrus*
Colt's-foot, purple *Homogyne alpina*
Cotoneaster, wild *Cotoneaster integerrimus*
Cottongrass, slender *Eriophorum gracile*
Cow-wheat, field *Melampyrum arvense*
Crocus, sand *Romulea columnae*
Cudweed, Jersey *Gnaphalium luteoalbum*
Cudweed, red-tipped *Filago lutescens*
Diapensia *Diapensia lapponica*
Eryngo, field *Eryngium campestre*
Fern, Killarney *Trichomanes speciosum*
Fleabane, Alpine *Erigeron borealis*
Fleabane, small *Pulicaria vulgaris*
Galingale, brown *Cyperus fuscus*
Gentian, Alpine *Gentiana nivalis*
Gentian, fringed *Gentianella ciliata*
Gentian, spring *Gentiana verna*
Germander, cut-leaved *Teucrium botrys*
Germander, water *Teucrium scordium*
Gladiolus, wild *Gladiolus illyricus*
Goosefoot, stinking *Chenopodium vulvaria*
Grass-poly *Lythrum hyssopifolia*
Hare's-ear, sickle-leaved *Bupleurum falcatum*
Hare's-ear, small *Bupleurum baldense*
Hawk's-beard, stinking *Crepis foetida*
Heath, blue *Phyllodoce caerulea*
Helleborine, red *Cephalanthera rubra*
Helleborine, Young's *Epipactis youngiana*
Horsetail, branched *Equisetum ramosissimum*
Hound's tongue, green *Cynoglossum germanicum*
Knawel, perennial *Scleranthus perennis*
Knotgrass, sea *Polygonum maritimum*
Lady's slipper *Cypripedium calceolus*
Lavender, rock sea- *Limonium paradoxum/Limonium recurvum*
Leek, round-headed *Allium sphaerocephalon*

Lettuce, least *Lactuca saligna*
Lily, Snowdon *Lloydia serotina*
Marsh-mallow, rough *Althaea hirsuta*
Marshwort, creeping *Apium repens*
Milk-parsley, Cambridge *Selinum carvifolia*
Naiad, holly-leaved *Najas marina*
Pennyroyal *Mentha pulegium*
Pigmyweed *Crassula aquatica*
Pink, Cheddar *Dianthus gratianopolitanus*
Pink, chidling *Petrorhagia nanteuilii*
Orchid, early spider- *Ophrys sphegodes*
Orchid, fen *Liparis loeselii*
Orchid, ghost *Epipogium aphyllum*
Orchid, late spider- *Ophrys fuciflora*
Orchid, lizard *Himantoglossum hircinum*
Orchid, military *Orchis militaris*
Orchid, monkey *Orchis simia*
Pear, Plymouth *Pyrus cordata*
Ragwort, fen *Senecio paludosus*
Ramping-fumitory, Martin's *Fumaria martinii*
Restharrow, small *Ononis reclinata*
Rock-cress, Alpine *Arabis alpina*
Rock-cress, Bristol *Arabis stricta*
Sandwort, Norwegian *Arenaria norvegica*
Sandwort, Teesdale *Minuartia stricta*
Saxifrage, drooping *Saxifraga cernua*
Saxifrage, tufted *Saxifraga cespitosa*
Solomon's-seal, whorled *Polygonatum verticillatum*
Sow-thistle, Alpine *Cicerbita alpina*
Speedwell, fingered *Veronica triphyllos*
Speedwell, spiked *Veronica spicata*
Spurge, purple *Euphorbia peplis*
Star-of-Bethlehem, early *Gagea bohemica*
Starfruit *Damasonium alisma*
Stonewort, foxtail *Lamprothamnium papulosum*
Strapwort *Corrigiola litoralis*
Violet, fen *Viola persicifolia*
Viper's-grass *Scorzonera humilis*
Water-plantain, ribbon-leaved *Alisma gramineum*
Wood-sedge, starved *Carex depauperata*
Woodsia, Alpine *Woodsia alpina*
Woodsia, oblong *Woodsia ilvensis*
Wormwood, field *Artemisia campestris*
Woundwort, limestone *Stachys alpina*
Woundwort, downy *Stachys germanica*
Yellow-rattle, greater *Rhinanthus serotinus*

First published 1988

Search Press Ltd
Wellwood, North Farm Road, Tunbridge Wells, Kent.
TN2 3DR

This book has been abridged from *The Miniature World of Pressed Flowers* by Nona Pettersen, published by Search Press Ltd in 1986.

ISBN 0 85532 625 5

Nona Pettersen was educated at St Gabriel's Convent School near Newbury and at St Marylebone High Street School in London. She now runs, with her husband and her mother, The Farriers Arms in Worcester, as well as a jewellery business with a strong interest in alternative materials.

She describes herself as having "the mentality of a magpie let loose in a flea market". While this does suggest something of her versatility – she has written about wine-making, a wide range of arts and crafts, not to mention confectionery, astrology and antique jewellery – it scarcely does justice to the extraordinary delicacy and skill of her miniature flower arrangements, many of which are shown in *The Miniature World of Pressed Flowers*.

Typeset by Phoenix Photosetting, Chatham, Kent
Printed in Italy by Amadeus S.P.A. Rome